Original title:
Beneath the Pear Tree

Copyright © 2025 Creative Arts Management OÜ
All rights reserved.

Author: Penelope Hawthorne
ISBN HARDBACK: 978-1-80586-392-2
ISBN PAPERBACK: 978-1-80586-864-4

Soliloquy of the Stillness

In the quiet, a squirrel prances,
Chasing a breeze, oh, what advances!
A bird chuckles, twirls in the air,
Pondering if it's time to share.

The grass whispers, a ticklish tease,
While ants march on, with such great ease.
"Who needs a throne?" one bug exclaims,
"We're royalty in our tiny games!"

The Fruitful Holiday

Under the sun, the fruits all grin,
Grapes binge-watch, while lemons spin.
"Fruits unite!" the apple shouts,
As peaches giggle, rolling about.

A watermelon jokes, "I'm a big slice!"
"Not as big as me!" cried out the rice.
They plan a feast with laughter and cheer,
Until the cat swoops in—oh dear!

Lullabies in the Glades

The crickets hum a cozy tune,
While frogs serenade under the moon.
A toadstool band plays sweet and soft,
As owls hoot, mysteriously aloft.

The fireflies dance, bright lights in flow,
"Watch my whirl!" one tiny spark goes.
The night chuckles, with mischief so sly,
"Who needs sleep? Let's just fly high!"

An Abode of Upturned Faces

Under the sky, all eyes look up,
A raccoon ponders, "Who drank my cup?"
The daisies giggle in a row,
While dandelions flaunt in the glow.

A wind-stirred breeze twists hats askew,
"Who wore it best?" the tulips coo.
With laughter erupting from earth to sky,
Even the clouds are wondering why!

Savoring the Sweetness of Solitude

In the shade I find my glee,
With snacks and laughter, just for me.
Ducks suggest I share my treat,
But my ice cream's far too sweet!

The world outside is bustling loud,
But here I'm happy, oh so proud.
A squirrel spies my cookie jar,
I just might share, won't go too far!

The Lure of the Juicy Drip

When fruits drip down in morning dew,
A sticky mess—oh what a view!
I chase the flavors, one by one,
Hoping today I'll finally run!

The ants march in with sugar dreams,
Plotting on how to steal my cream.
I guard my snacks, I take my stand,
While they conspire, oh, so grand!

Memories Locked Within the Boughs

Old tales hang from every leaf,
Like whispers sweet, beyond belief.
The giggles of a summer's day,
Echo where we used to play.

I roam and search for signs of fun,
Like every fruit that's come and spun.
A hidden stash, a secret place,
Where memories giggle in the space.

Amidst the Lushness of Life's Gifts

Among the greens, I laugh and scoff,
At random bugs who try to puff.
With every bite, I'm filled with cheer,
Life's comedy is crystal clear!

From gentle leaves to squishy spills,
Nature brings laughter, endless thrills.
The fruit parade is quite a sight,
In this garden, everything feels right!

Stories Woven in Petals

A squirrel with a hat so grand,
Danced beneath the branches, quite unplanned.
He slipped on dew, took quite a fall,
Then laughed it off, with a cheeky call.

The petals giggled, the breeze did tease,
While bees wore sunglasses, buzzing with ease.
Each flower told tales of wobbly strides,
In a garden where whimsy freely glides.

Pathways of Dappled Sunshine

A cat in shades lounged on a beam,
Dreaming of fish swimming upstream.
The shadows danced, the light did play,
As a rabbit skidded, in a wobbly way.

With sunshine giggles bouncing around,
The daisies chuckled, all safe and sound.
A frog croaked jokes, just for fun,
While a lazy lizard rather basked in the sun.

Gifts of Nature's Kindness

A butterfly wore a tutu so bright,
Flitting and fluttering, quite the sight.
While ants carried crumbs in a little parade,
Laughing together, plans poorly laid.

A worm popped up, seeking a friend,
Said, "Want to dig? Or just pretend?"
With laughter echoing through the ground,
Nature's antics cheerfully abound.

The Essence of Earthly Connections

A hedgehog with glasses read a book,
While a deer peeked in, with a curious look.
"Is that a mystery, or just a tale?"
The hedgehog chuckled, "It's about a snail!"

A breeze whooshed by, carrying jokes,
As tiny fairies chuckled, stirring the oaks.
Under the leafy canopy so grand,
Life's oddball moments—all perfectly planned.

The Scent of Hidden Bliss

In shadows cool where secrets dwell,
A jester's laugh, a ringing bell.
With mischief wrapped in fruit's disguise,
We plot and scheme, beneath the skies.

A stinky sock, an apple's peer,
The tales of laughter, loud and clear.
Crisp crunches echo, biting glee,
A comical feast, come share with me.

Legacy in Every Fallen Leaf

Each leaf that tumbles, spins a laugh,
A leafy wig, the wind's own staff.
With every twirl, a grand charade,
The history of our masquerade.

We toss our woes like leaves in flight,
A shower of giggles, pure delight.
Every crinkle tells a joke,
As memories dance, the silence broke.

A Canopy of Nostalgia

Up high they sway, the branches tease,
A throne for squirrels, a joke with ease.
With nutty banter from furry friends,
The laughter echoes, it never ends.

Under this roof of giggles bright,
We share our jests till autumn's night.
With every nut a hidden prank,
The stories swirl in laughter's bank.

Rituals of the Fruitful Dawn

At dawn we gather, ready to cheer,
With breakfast fruit, we hold it dear.
Bananas dance, oranges sing,
As morning calls, we take to wing.

A fruity feast, the sunlight glows,
With every bite, our humor flows.
The crunch of joy, the squeeze of zest,
In this bright laughter, we're truly blessed.

The Glistening Fruits Above

Up in the branches, fruits swing high,
Aiming for mouths but oh, they fly!
Chasing a balance, a tumble, a pout,
My lunch just waved and then it took out.

The squirrels are plotting, their eyes all aglow,
With plans to outsmart us, just watch the show!
One grabs a pear, and a second lets loose,
While I sit below in my lunch-time recluse.

Rainsong on Sweet Wood

The raindrops dance on leaves with a plink,
Making a symphony that makes you think!
Each puddle sings tales of slippery cheer,
And socks that get drenched, well, that's what I fear.

With umbrellas like boats, we navigate streams,
While laughing at puddles and joking our dreams.
A splash here and there, suddenly surprised,
We'll call it a bath, 'cause who's going to mind?

A Nest of Dreams

Look to the branches, it's quite a sight,
A nest of ideas takes wing in flight!
With birds that cackle and chirp silly tunes,
While I try to nap under afternoon's moons.

Daydreams of flying while they silly scream,
I join in their chorus, it's all quite the theme!
With feathers as pillows, I snooze for a while,
Awakening only when I hear their wild smile.

The Shade of Forgotten Tales

In the cool of the shade, with stories to share,
Old folks recounting, with laughter in air.
Once there was a thief who stole all the pies,
And a cat that wore glasses, oh, what a surprise!

The stories grow taller, as shadows align,
Of dragons, and mischief, and pickle brine.
With punchlines like arrows, they hit all the marks,
As we sit in delight, counting up all the quarks.

A Nest of Petals

In a garden of mismatched shoes,
Butterflies dance, sipping on dews.
A squirrel steals a single bloom,
While daisies chuckle in their room.

One rose blushed at a bee's cheeky tease,
Said, 'My perfume is meant to please!'
But the bee buzzed off, too busy for flair,
Leaving the rose in a snippy despair.

The Quiescent Prayer of Seeds

Little seeds huddle in cozy rows,
Whispering dreams of future grows.
One said, 'I'll be a pumpkin so bright!'
Another giggled, 'I'll be a delight!'

They plotted their rise with glee and jest,
Laughing at flowers, 'We're the best!'
But when sprouting time finally arrived,
They tripped in the mud, surprisingly revived.

Fruits of Labor

A banana slipped on its own peel,
Yelling, 'This isn't a fair deal!'
An apple laughed, 'You should look where you land!'
As grapes rolled by, just too grand.

Plums were plotting a fruit parade,
While cherries giggled, in shadows they played.
They danced and rolled across the grass,
But fell in a pile, a fruity mass!

Sheltered Secrets

Under leaves, a secret meeting planned,
Where the critters all took a stand.
A rabbit sneezed, and all went still,
'I'm allergic to the grass, what a thrill!'

An owl hooted, 'Keep your voices low!'
While a fox said, 'Let's put on a show!'
But a hedgehog snorted, losing its cool,
'Planning is fine, but let's not be fools!'

Under the Canopy of Time

Time rolled by, with a mischievous grin,
Hiding away where the laughter begins.
Coconuts dropped, with a thud to the ground,
While the leaves all whispered, 'Did you hear that sound?'

A turtle declared, 'I do not rush!'
As a rabbit zipped past in a hush.
They laughed at the sun, a lazy old thing,
Turning the world into a playful fling.

Beneath the Blossoms' Veil

In the shade where giggles bloom,
The bees play tag, avoiding doom.
A squirrel dances, quite a sight,
His acorn hat is just so right.

We share a laugh with every breeze,
As blossoms whisper silly pleas.
Nature's joke, oh what a scheme,
A fruit salad in a wild dream.

The Silent Poetry of Sweetness

With every step, we tread on dreams,
Dancing through the twirling beams.
A ladybug with painted grace,
Winks at us with a cheeky face.

Among the fruits, we spot a clown,
Wobbling by in a fruit-skin gown.
His laughter echoes, a joyous sound,
In this berry patch, we're spellbound.

A Dance Among the Falling Petals

Petals land like confetti drops,
Making hats on our silly tops.
The puppies chase as squirrels snicker,
A garden party? Yes, much quicker!

We twirl and spin, in shades of pink,
Wonder what the neighbors think.
The sun peeks through, a knowing grin,
It's always fun when chaos wins!

Hidden Beneath the Canopy

Under cover where critters play,
Lizards do the cha-cha, hooray!
Frolicsome shadows, jump and cheer,
As wise old owls drink root beer.

A picnic spread, it's quite a sight,
Plus sandwiches that don't quite fight.
The juice spills over, a fruity flood,
Our joyous mess, nature's good bud.

Reflecting in a Pool of Shade

In the dappled light, I sit,
With squirrels planning their great skit.
A dance of shadows, laughter calls,
As green grass teases my bare toes' falls.

The sun spots play hide and seek,
While ants march by, all looking sleek.
I think I saw a crow in a hat,
But maybe it's just my old cat.

Beneath the Fragrant Canopy

A breeze slips through the leafy maze,
And I find myself in a fragrant daze.
The bees are buzzing with gossip and cheer,
While I munch on cookies, they eye my beer.

A worm wiggles up with a wobbly grin,
Says, "Let's dance a jig, I'll show you how to spin!"
The flowers giggle and sway in the bright,
Laughing at ants having a late-night fight.

The Timeworn Branches Speak

Old branches creak, they have stories to share,
About cheeky robins who ruffled their hair.
They chuckle and whisper of years gone by,
How the wind tickles leaves, making them sigh.

A raccoon tried to climb, dressed up like a thief,
But slipped and fell off like a clumsy leaf.
The laughter echoes from trunk to trunk,
As the smell of ripe fruit gets us all sunk.

Sanctuary of the Sun-Drenched Earth

Here in this realm, where sunlight beams,
We giggle at geese prepping for schemes.
A picnic blanket adorned with crumbs,
While nearby frogs croak the day's cute hums.

Kids run wild, their laughter a delight,
While bees throw parties in their honeybite.
The world tilts slightly, in this cozy spot,
Where silly moments are cherished a lot.

Whispers of Succulent Shadows

In the shadow's soft chatters,
Fruits giggle in playful tones,
Bouncing in wind's gentle tattle,
While ants march in silly zones.

A squirrel dons a quirky hat,
Chasing dreams of acorn pies,
Beneath leafy clumps, he sat,
Winking with mischievous eyes.

Secrets in the Orchard's Embrace

The apples plot a silly scheme,
Whispering tales full of zest,
To juice or not? A fruity dream,
In their tartness, lies their jest.

Pears with laughter roll about,
Making jokes about old seeds,
While bees buzz in to check it out,
Dancing round like jolly breeds.

The Gravity of Ripened Dreams

Oh, how the ripe ones tend to fall,
No warning given, just a plop!
They seem to giggle, have a ball,
As they tumble, they never stop.

A dream of pie, they twist and tease,
While worms plot their great escape,
In every fruit, a riddle brews,
As nature bends, we dance and gape.

Echoes in the Fruit-Laden Canopy

Laughter hints in branches high,
Where the fruits dare to exchange,
A peach's wink, a pear's sly sigh,
In the midst of playful change.

With each rustle, a joke is shared,
The melon rolls, the plum makes quips,
Underneath, the ground prepared,
For giggles found in juicy drips.

Flickers of Sunset Through Green

The sun dips low, a squinting eye,
Squirrels in shades wave goodbye.
Each leaf a stage for acorn jokes,
While shadows dance, the laughter pokes.

A rabbit hops, with flair and grace,
Wearing a hat, it joins the race.
The grass giggles, tickled by feet,
As the evening air tastes bittersweet.

Crickets chirp, their lines on cue,
While fireflies audition, just a few.
The breeze carries whispers of cheer,
In this green stage, good times are near.

We gather round, friends lost in play,
Between the roots, we laugh and sway.
In this twilight, each giggle's gold,
Nature's comedy forever told.

A Palette of Nature's Best

With colors bright and laughter loud,
A painter's stroke, nature's crowd.
The daisies dance in polka dot shoes,
While sunflowers boast their golden views.

A butterfly sets its wings to spin,
Chasing its shadow on a whim.
"Tag, you're it!" shouts a bumblebee,
In this garden of glee, all are free.

The mud pies baked by cheeky toes,
In the shade, the mischief grows.
With giggles burst, and spatters of fun,
We close our day as adventures run.

The palette shifts as twilight falls,
The crickets echo, nature calls.
With colors fading, laughter stays,
In this scheme of joy, forever plays.

Stirring the Roots of Yesterday

A tree once whispered tales of old,
Of chipmunks bold and beans that scold.
The roots recall with hearty cheer,
As we climb high and shed a tear.

Memories peek from leafy beds,
Of puns exchanged and silly threads.
A gopher laughs, "A nut you dropped!"
While daisies cheer, "You should have hopped!"

The sun's embrace wraps us tight,
In this playful, golden light.
We toss our doubts to the winds' fuss,
Hand in hand, creating a fuss.

With every laugh, the past revives,
In this green zone, laughter thrives.
Tomorrow waits with tales anew,
In roots of tomorrow, laughter grew.

The Heart of Abundant Green

In playful shades of emerald hue,
Joy blossoms bright, where fun comes too.
The jovial leaves with whispers shared,
In this land of laughter, none are spared.

A frolicsome breeze teases the grass,
As ants wear capes and prance with sass.
They hold a meeting, they take a stand,
In this lively place, it's all well planned.

Underneath a giggling sky,
Clouds tickle the joy drifting by.
We chase the sparkles, hand in hand,
In the heart of green, jests so grand.

The evening sings a funny tune,
Fireflies rave with the rising moon.
While shadows play, the night's agleam,
In abundant cheer, we chase the dream.

A Tapestry of Green and Gold

In a garden wild, not quite a dream,
Lemons chat loudly, or so they seem.
Mangoes wiggle, trying to boast,
While broccoli hides behind a toast.

The daisies critique the sun's glowing light,
While carrots gossip, full of delight.
The squirrels act like they own the spot,
But no one admits they like it a lot.

Tomatoes blush when the breeze comes near,
And pumpkins giggle, holding back cheer.
Each veggie's tale brings joy to the day,
In this patch of laughter, they joke and play.

When moonlight sneaks in, shadows do dance,
As zucchini prances, taking a chance.
They whisper and chatter until the dawn,
This lively garden, a riot of fun.

The Rustling Cadence

Leaves are a-frolic, wafting in air,
As acorns tumble without a care.
Chickens debate who'll reign as queen,
While roosters strut, oh, proud and keen.

A breeze joins the laughter, swirling around,
As nature jests without making a sound.
The sun starts to wink, making its play,
Chasing around flowers that sway and sway.

Bees buzz in rhythm, so cheerful and bold,
In this bustling scene, laughter unfolds.
The earth wears smiles in shades of bright green,
Creating a canvas that's never routine.

With every rustle, there's humor at play,
Nature's chorus in a grand ballet.
Join in the fun, don't stand too still,
In the whirl of the garden, there's joy to fulfill.

Memories Linger Here

In this spot where whispers of laughter bloom,
A dog named Barkley finds room to zoom.
Squirrels in a race, who'll claim the prize?
While frogs leap about, to nature's surprise.

Dandelions giggle, spitting their seeds,
While butterflies dodge in their playful deeds.
A cat yawns loudly, claiming the sun,
As shadows skedaddle, having their fun.

Each twig tells a story, cracked and dry,
As old leaves collect tales from the sky.
The blooms laugh together, sharing their stance,
In this patch of happiness, all join the dance.

Time drifts like clouds, but the joy is clear,
As memories linger, they persevere.
In this garden of mirth, we all feel linked,
Where every giggle is perfectly sync'd.

Darkness and Light in Harmony

As shadows stretch, whispers of cheer,
Frogs serenade the night, crystal clear.
The moon shares secrets with clouds overhead,
While starlit giggles play in the thread.

Crickets compose their symphonies bright,
While owls chuckle under the cover of night.
The fireflies dance in a twinkling spree,
Winking and blinking, so carefree.

As shadows shiver, the sun takes a peek,
Painting the world in a playful streak.
The contrast of light, it stirs the mind,
With humor and jest, a bond that's entwined.

In this lively space, darkness meets light,
Where laughter unfurls, banishing fright.
Together they thrive, in magical play,
In the garden of jokes, brightening the day.

The Secret Life of Ripening Pears

In the quiet yard, they wiggle and sway,
Hoping to drop, but no one will play.
Whispering secrets of sweetened delight,
Dreaming of pies and a warm, cozy night.

They giggle and wiggle, all round and green,
Pondering life as the stars intervene.
"Who'll pick us first?" is a question they pose,
As flies buzz around, giving everyone woes.

With the sun's golden rays, they bask with a cheer,
Counting the days 'til their harvest is near.
A tickle of dew drapes the gang overhead,
While squirrels sneak off with the last slice of bread.

A dance of the branches, what fun to behold,
With each gust of wind, more tales to be told.
Oh how they prance in this summer's affair,
Chasing the laughter that floats through the air.

Shadows Dancing in Eden's Keep

In a garden of dreams where shadows play tricks,
There's a crew out to munch on the earth's finest picks.
Happiness blooms in a light-hearted game,
While butterflies gossip and giggle in fame.

With tosses of petals, and soft rustling leaves,
A squirrel plays tag through the canopies' eaves.
Whispers of fruit, a mischievous feast,
As the breeze sways the branches, the laughter increased.

Beneath veils of green, little critters unite,
As they prance in the shadows, oh what a sight!
The rustle of fun keeps the worries afar,
While the moon peeks in, shining down like a star.

So gather 'round, you dear dancers of glee,
In this orchard of madness, come join the spree.
For life is a play in the soft evening glow,
Where shadows and laughter forever will flow.

Shadows of Lush Canopy

Beneath heavy branches, the fun never ends,
With winking-eyed critters and whimsical friends.
They skitter and scamper, they leap with delight,
Sharing the mischief that gleams through the night.

A party of shadows, the fun to unfold,
With stories of joy that beg to be told.
In the shade they all gather, to dance and to feast,
Echoing laughter, both lively and least.

Plump fruit teases on branches held high,
While the breeze carries giggles, sweet as a pie.
In a chorus of chirps, there's a grand celebration,
An orchard of jokes, with no reservation.

As the sun melts away, and the stars take their stage,
The critters all chuckle, they come of age.
In the garden of whispers, oh how they thrive,
Beneath lush canopies, where shadows survive.

The Whispering Leaves

The leaves chattered softly, in a giggly spree,
They spoke of the ants, plotting a grand jubilee.
Squirrels stood by, trying to catch the scoop,
While the birds dropped notes, forming a funny troupe.

The breeze joined in, with a sneaky little sway,
As if to say, "Isn't this a quirky day?"
A cheese-loving mouse, with a wink and a nod,
Scooted by quickly, pretending to be God.

Laughter erupted from the cluster so green,
As bugs told stories, perfectly unseen.
They shared tales of raindrops and mischief in air,
Every ripple of joy, a joke beyond compare.

Oh, to be near where the silliness thrives,
In the whispers and giggles of leaf-laden lives.
For in that cool shade, so bright and so queer,
Nature's snickers echo, so full of good cheer.

Secrets of the Orchard

In the orchard's heart, where drunks bid adieu,
A fox lost his glasses, oh what a hullabaloo!
He searched under branches, with a zeal so profound,
Only to find them in a peach's round crown.

The pears laughed aloud, their glee hard to hide,
As the fox blushed crimson, with naught but his pride.
"What's this? Am I losing my pantless charm?"
The jests of the fruits, they raised quite the alarm!

A turtle, slow-moving, took part in this jest,
Claiming he's fast, when he's simply the best.
His shell was a cruiser, an yonder ship's fate,
He'd challenge the winds to a fateful debate.

Cherry blossoms joined with a giggle and cheer,
While the lemons rolled in with a zesty sneer.
And with every bloom, all mischief took flight,
In the orchard where secrets danced into the night.

Dance of the Falling Fruits

Apples rolled down, in a grand fruit parade,
They twirled and they spun, in their colorful robes displayed.
Bananas stood by, forming a conga line,
While pears started giggling, all feeling divine.

Out came the oranges, with zest in their sway,
They tripped on their peels, what a messy ballet!
Strawberries blushed as they watched from afar,
They giggled and tossed, oh what a bizarre.

Grapes joined the fun, bouncing here and there,
"Watch this," they shouted, "we'll throw flair in the air!"
As laughter erupted, it echoed abroad,
With fruits in full frolic, so joyous, so proud.

And when sunset fell, with a soft, golden hue,
Each fruit knew the laughter was a beautiful cue.
In the orchard they danced, till the moon took its place,
With smiles that lingered, in this cheerful space.

Echoes Under the Boughs

Under leafy shadows, the acorns played tricks,
With echoes of laughter, they formed silly clicks.
"Oh, look at that squirrel, so puffed and so grand,
With a sandwich in paws, thinking he's well-planned!"

The breeze whispered stories of wobbling stems,
As old branches chuckled like raucous gems.
"One day I'll grow hair," a young nut said with a glee,
While each leaf above danced, wild and free.

Beneath arching limbs, where bright shadows blend,
A bunch of old ciders would continually mend,
The ruckus they made, stirred the spirits around,
In every good giggle, fresh joy could be found.

So here's to the whispers, the chuckles they share,
To the fruits and their tales, so joyful and rare.
In the echoes that bounce, where each laughter rings,
Life under the boughs makes the merriest things.

Unraveled Threads of Nature's Tapestry

In a garden where fruit takes a nap,
Squirrels dance in a sticky sap.
A worm named Fred wears a tiny hat,
While bees sip tea, how about that?

The petals giggle, they tickle the breeze,
Rabbits boast of their leafy degrees.
A chicken struts with a crown of corn,
Claiming the title of 'Fruity Morn.'

The sun throws shade on the playful vine,
Where tomatoes plot to sip on wine.
Mice wear shoes from last autumn's stash,
While carrots join in with a dash of flash.

Laughter rings through the jolly leaves,
As nature's party never leaves.
A dance of figs to a squirrel's glee,
In this wild, silly jubilee!

The Lullaby of Orchard Shadows

Underneath the giggling green,
A shadow weaves a funny scene.
Chickens hum a sleepy tune,
While apples plot their afternoon.

A goat with glasses reads the news,
While the grass throws a wild snooze.
A cat in gloves plays a trick,
On the mice who take it slow and slick.

Lemons roll in a silly race,
With cherries trying to keep pace.
In this lullaby of silly sounds,
Edible laughter joyfully abounds.

As twilight spills its golden gleam,
The foliage winks, quite the dream.
A soirée blooms as stars ignite,
In nature's whimsy, pure delight!

Enigmas in the Edible Canopy

In a canopy, secrets abound,
Berries giggle without a sound.
A parrot sings the fruit's fair song,
While nutty squirrels dance along.

Peaches wear socks, quite the trend,
While giggling grapes around them bend.
Broccoli acts quite mature,
As carrots giggle, they feel unsure.

A turnip dons a funny face,
Challenging radishes to a race.
Funny things float in this sky,
Where humor and harvest fly high.

As twilight whispers funny tales,
The moon joins in, leaving trails.
With puns and laughter everywhere,
In this edible wonder, who would dare?

Reveries of the Lush Undergrowth

In lush realms where the ferns have fun,
Snails zoom by, their race begun.
A hedgehog juggles berries with flair,
While daisies gossip without a care.

Frogs leap high, trying for gold,
While mushrooms share jokes, quite bold.
Worms in bow ties break the mold,
As sunbeams sprinkle, stories unfold.

From tree to root, whispers roll,
A riotous laughter fills the whole.
A dragonfly hosts a comedy night,
In the roots where shadows alight.

As dusk approaches, giggles abound,
In the wild where joy is found.
Nature's jesters take their stage,
In the tales of the leafy page!

A Symphony of Sweet Fragrance

The bees are buzzing with delight,
Gathering nectar, oh what a sight!
A dance of pollen in the air,
Those little whiskers with utmost flair.

Butterflies flit and then they pause,
Admiring blooms, because they can!
A scented serenade, my nose does boast,
With laughter, I toast my floral host!

The fruits are plump, so juicy, so round,
Each one a treasure waiting to be found.
I take a bite, and with sticky hands,
I laugh aloud at my fruity plans!

Nature's giggle, a merry tune,
Laughter, like sunlight, makes me swoon.
In this fragrant kingdom, absurdity reigns,
As I revel in sweetness, and ignore the stains.

Memories in the Soil

Digging deep with a curious shovel,
What treasures hide in this garden hovel?
A shoe, a toy, maybe a bone,
Echoes of laughter, all on their own.

I plant my seeds with hopes of gold,
But squirrels have plans, they're oh so bold!
They dig and they dance, what mischief they make,
I swear, they're planning a nutty earthquake!

Each sprout's a story that begs to be told,
Garden gnomes chuckle, their secrets unfold.
Who knew mud could bring such a grin?
As I slip and slide, I'm losing my win!

The worms are wiggling, making a scene,
It's a wriggly party that's fit for a queen.
With every turn of my gardening feat,
I find that the laughter is hard to beat!

Hidden Beneath Greenery

Under the leaves where shadows play,
A sneaky fox sleeps through the day.
But wait, what's this? A picnic spread,
He sniffs the air and he's out of bed!

The ants march on like a tiny parade,
While I sip lemonade, feeling quite laid.
But under my toes, oh what a surprise,
They're plotting a feast, oh what a guise!

A little bird tweets a gossip so loud,
It tickles my ear, makes me laugh proud.
What tales do they weave from up in the tree?
I bet it involves squirrels, just wait and see!

The grass is a carpet, soft and inviting,
Where laughter and mischief keep all uniting.
As I roll and I tumble, ever so free,
Nature's a jester, amusing for me!

Embrace of the Swaying Branches

The branches sway with a friendly grin,
As I approach with my giant kin.
They tickle my hair, oh what a tease!
I dance around, oh how they please!

The fruit above, it's a tempting lure,
But swinging low, it's a fruit we're sure!
I reach and stumble, with laughter I fall,
Green apples giggle, oh, they have it all!

I kick at the ground, feeling quite spry,
While peas sprout above, they wave me goodbye.
With vines that twirl and twigs that sway,
I find my joy in this leafy ballet!

The air is a concert, sweet wind and glee,
A rustling chorus, nature's decree.
With every sway, every giggling breeze,
I revel in laughter, delightful with ease!

Ripeness in the Still Air

The fruits just hang, so round and ripe,
Their laughter spills in every type.
A squirrel plots with acorn chest,
While birds debate which snack is best.

A bee buzzes with royal flair,
Dancing round without a care.
He slips and flips, a clumsy fool,
In nature's waltz, he breaks the rule.

The wind it whispers, jokes they share,
Tickling grass with gentle flair.
A sun-kissed day, so full of glee,
Let's toast the shade with iced sweet tea.

As laughter echoes, roots hold tight,
To nature's play, a pure delight.
And though the fruits may start to fall,
The joy they bring outshines it all.

Guardian of the Garden

There stands a gnome with a painted grin,
He guards the blooms and the chaos within.
With tiny arms and a pointy hat,
He shouts, "No pests; get off my mat!"

The weeds they giggle, plotting schemes,
While flowers sway in sunlight beams.
The gnome, he winks, with a silent cheer,
"Not on my watch, keep that a leer!"

The ladybug dons a tiny cape,
While slugs request a little shape.
A grumpy hedgehog snubs his nose,
"Why can't these critters just wear clothes?"

The garden's realm, a wild dance,
With gnome-like giggles at every chance.
A chorus blooms with every glance,
In this patch, there's always chance.

Sunlight's Caress on Tender Roots

The sunshine peeks through leafy green,
A ticklish touch, a morning scene.
Worms stretch out with a silly grin,
As praise flows in from roots within.

The petals stretch to catch a beam,
While shadows giggle, plotting dreams.
A timid sprout, so fresh and new,
Wonders if it can reach the blue.

The clouds they puff, a cheeky show,
As sunlight weaves through ground below.
With every beam, the laughter grows,
Filling the air, where one joy flows.

Tender roots in a playful race,
With earthworms sharing their funny space.
The dance of life, in soil so bright,
Together they twinkle with pure delight.

The Dance of Blossoms

In springtime's giggles, flowers sway,
Like children twirling at a play.
Petals giggle, colors in frolic,
In fragrant whispers, laughter's melodic.

A bee-bop bee goes round and round,
With pollen dreams on soft ground.
"Who's the best dancer?" flowers declare,
As blooms compete with flair so rare.

Their petals flutter in joyous flight,
Sunshine sparkles, hearts feel light.
Even the breeze takes time to prance,
In the garden's grand, blossomy dance.

As twilight falls, the blossoms hum,
A sleepy tune, a soft-hearted drum.
With nature's laughter and twilight tease,
The garden lays down, ready to freeze.

Underneath the Orchard's Gaze

In the shade, we eat our pies,
A squirrel steals with hungry eyes.
Laughter echoes, seeds take flight,
As fruit drops down—a comical sight.

A bee buzzed in, a wild affair,
Left me wondering where's my hair.
The apples grin, with faces bold,
We joke they might be turning old.

With each bite, a giggle spins,
"Is that a worm?" Oh, here it grins!
The juice drips down, a sweet cascade,
Wipe it quick, or it won't fade.

Yet still we sit, amid the fun,
Awaiting more—the day is young.
Under branches, shadows play,
We crown ourselves the kings of clay.

Musing in the Green Abyss

In the grass, we lost our shoes,
The ants march by, they have their dues.
A rabbit hops, he takes a glance,
As we attempt a silly dance.

With melons round and faces bright,
We chuckle at our silly plight.
A pickle jar, our prize today,
A snack we're sure won't go astray.

We ponder life, amidst the leaves,
While laughter's trickle never leaves.
Is that a bug, or just my hat?
We join the chase—oh, where's it at?

Out here, the world seems just so grand,
A picnic dream that's never planned.
With crumbs and smiles, we make a mess,
In this chaos, life's a funny guess.

Lost in the Garden's Embrace

Tangled vines, a playful maze,
Tomatoes roll in sunlit rays.
With pranks and jests, we weave our cheer,
Each corner hides a secret leer.

My hat's been stolen by a crow,
Chased it twice, but oh, so slow!
They squawk and caw, with such a flair,
A jest is worth, beyond compare!

The carrots giggle, snug in rows,
With every dig, my laughter grows.
A puddle gleams, a splashy art,
A jump, a laugh, it steals my heart.

Among the blooms, our stories weave,
Each tale is silly, just believe.
In nature's arms, we lose the frown,
Together here, we wear the crown.

The Gentle Sway of Time's Harvest

The apples sway in gentle tease,
With every breeze, they seem to sneeze.
We laugh, we run, we reach for more,
Each pluck a chance to start a war.

A ladder stands, quite wobbly too,
I climb with glee to get a view.
But oops, I slip, it's quite the show,
Like a fruit falling, down I go!

We gather round, the feast is set,
Pumpkin pie—now that's a bet!
The critters eye, our spoils to share,
With toothy grins, they join the fare.

Yet here amidst the fruity fun,
The laughter echoes, never shun.
In this delight, we count the stars,
Wishing on these silly jars.

Garden of Dreams and Secrets

In the garden where gnomes dance,
Squirrels plot their nutty romance,
Cabbages wear hats, quite absurd,
While talking frogs croak every word.

The flowers gossip, petals aflame,
They whisper secrets, tease their name,
A dandelion dreams of flight,
But ends up just a fuzzy sight.

Pumpkins rolling in playful jest,
Compete for the title of the best,
A sunflower winks at a bee,
"Join my dance, come buzz with me!"

Beneath the moon's playful glare,
Every creature finds a flair,
In this garden, laughter blooms,
As joy in every corner looms.

The Telling Quiet of Twilight

In twilight's hush, a bat took flight,
Mistook a hair for a tasty bite,
The sheep in woolly coats do laugh,
As night becomes a cheeky gaff.

Crickets tune their evening song,
Each note a note of life gone wrong,
A hedgehog trips, with quite a sound,
While fireflies play tag around.

The stars above snicker and gleam,
As frogs launch into their deep dream,
This evening circus is a sight,
Where shadows dance, both left and right.

In quiet moments filled with cheer,
We raise our glasses to night's veneer,
For every giggle hides a tale,
In the world where wonders prevail.

Rustling Tales of the Orchard

In the orchard, apples gossip loud,
They wear their red coats, feeling proud,
While pears don't mind, they just roll by,
Chasing the breeze, beneath the sky.

A scarecrow dreams of travel far,
While crows plan pranks with a sweet star,
"Oh, how'd you find that shiny thing?"
A wind-chime hangs, begins to sing.

Bees debate who's the best dancer,
Each buzz is a chance to romancer,
The cherries giggle in their own way,
As plums wish for a sunny day.

Underneath the leafy chatter,
Every harvest holds a scatter,
Of tales crafted from sunshine's art,
In laughter's echo, they take part.

Guardian of Time's Gifts

A clock in the garden ticks away,
While rabbits skip and play their way,
The sun's a friend, always on time,
As flowers bloom in rhythm and rhyme.

Old trees tell tales of days gone by,
With branches stretching to the sky,
While crickets count in beats so fine,
A heartbeat shared, yours and mine.

The breeze whispers moments, softly ticked,
While giggling leaves dance, slightly kicked,
Time keeps secrets in its sway,
Yet laughter holds them, keeps the day.

In every tick, in every chime,
Lies a riddle of space and time,
A playful pause, a gift to share,
In the garden, where joy hangs in the air.

Beneath the Old Wisteria

A squirrel in a hat, quite a sight,
Dancing on branches, oh what a bite!
With acorns in pockets, he juggles with glee,
While bees buzz along with sweet harmony.

The gardener sighs, all plans out the door,
As tomatoes go missing, he can't take much more.
The vines have conspired, a party so wild,
With rabbits doing tango, oh isn't it mild?

Jaybirds are laughing, the sun's taking notes,
As butterflies play the fool, wearing coats.
A picnic of giggles, with sandwiches rare,
As laughter erupts in that wild, fragrant air.

But who will come clean when the sun says goodbye?
The old wisteria whispers a chuckle, oh my!
"Dear friends, just remember, when chaos takes flight,
Even nature's a jester in the soft fading light."

The Last Light of Day's Embrace

The sun packs its bags, quite the show,
While fireflies twinkle, saying hello.
A chicken in slippers, it's left in a flap,
Clucks serenading the twilight's soft tap.

Cats play cards, trying to bluff,
"Only one treat? Surely that's tough!"
While a mouse makes a dash for a crumb on the floor,
The world's turned into a sitcom, who could ask for more?

A dog wearing glasses reads under the tree,
With a sigh, he reflects, "Life's just too free."
As shadows stretch long, the laughter ignites,
In the last light of day, friendships take flights.

So gather your friends, let the giggles unfold,
The night's just beginning with wonders untold.
In the embrace of dusk, let's dance and let sway,
For in moments like these, we laugh all the way.

Aroma of Dappled Sunshine

Dandelions giggle as they sprout from the ground,
In a race with the butterflies swirling around.
A dog with a donut sits slack-jawed in bliss,
While ants hold a meeting, plotting for this.

The aroma is laughing, it tickles the nose,
"Who knew grass could sing? Oh, the joy it bestows!"
A squirrel flips pancakes, a chef in disguise,
While the sun nods along, painting laughs in the skies.

Now picnics are served up with lemonade cheer,
As ants in tuxedos bring laughter near.
A watermelon burst, a party's begun,
In every bright corner, shines warmth from the sun.

So let's gather our giggles, let the fun never fade,
In this magical moment, let memories cascade.
For the aroma of sunshine wraps kisses 'round tight,
As we share in the joy, from morning to night.

Shadows Caught in a Dream

A shadow with shoes starts tapping away,
While a squirrel brings nuts for the late matinee.
As clouds wear their fluff like a jolly old friend,
These shadows are giggling, oh, when will it end?

With acorns for trumpets, they all join the band,
While frogs leap in rhythm, oh, isn't it grand?
A raccoon tries singing, but oh what a croak!
In this concert of whimsy, it's laughter, not yoke.

As twilight approaches, in swirls of delight,
The shadows are twirling, in the soft fading light.
They twine through the grass, swirling high on a beam,
All caught in the moment, lost in a dream.

So if you should wander, remember this scene,
Of shadows in laughter, where giggles convene.
In the glow of the moonlight, let joy take its flight,
For life is much sweeter in shadows of light.

Songs of Growth and Burden

In the garden, a plant's grand dream,
Roots are tangled, bursting at the seam.
Leaves are laughing, stretching for the sky,
While the worms wiggle, asking, 'Oh, why?'

Each blossom blooms with a cheeky grin,
Chasing the sun, where the fun begins.
But wait, oh no! The rain starts to pour,
And the puddles plead for a dance on the floor.

A squirrel prances, stealing a bite,
"That's my harvest!" I shout in fright.
They giggle and scamper, the thieves of delight,
While I scheme to catch them tonight.

At the end of the day, I take a seat,
Leaves above wave, say, "We've got you beat!"
In this circus of greens, laughter's the key,
Life's a comedy, can't you see?

The Pulse of Hidden Sweetness

In the orchard, a secret waits to bloom,
With whispers of fruit in the leafy room.
Jokes between branches, they tease and they poke,
With a twist of fate, the birds start to croak.

An apple winks, "I'm sweeter than pie!"
While the grapes giggle, swaying close by.
A plump little peach, with a chuckle so grand,
"Watch out for the ants, they form quite a band!"

The shadows sway with a dose of flair,
As bees buzz around without a care.
"Hey, wait for me!" the flowers all shout,
Sipping the sunshine like a drink to tout.

In this sweet circus, no moment's the same,
Growth is a song, and fruit's just a game.
With laughter and spritz, our harvest's a feast,
Beneath the fun, sweetness never ceased.

Life's Bounty Above and Below

In the soil, the roots play hide and seek,
While above, the branches giggle and squeak.
"Are you there?" questions a cheeky old vine,
"Just look for the fruit, you're sure to find mine!"

Sunflowers sway, throwing shade on the scene,
"Life's too short to pout, just dance like a queen!"
So the carrots chuckle, wearing dirt with pride,
As a tumbleweed spins, joining in on the ride.

The harvest whispers, "We're ripe for a feast!"
And the scurrying critters come out for a beast.
"Not so fast, my friends!" I laugh with delight,
As they all scramble, what a hilarious sight!

From the earth to the sky, a party ensues,
With every new sprout sharing daytime views.
Life blossoms wildly, with funny turns galore,
In this garden of laughter, who could ask for more?

A Tapestry of Leaves and Fruit

In the patch, color spins a tale so bright,
Where leaves chuckle softly as day turns to night.
"Pluck me if you dare!" a berry dares to say,
While the pumpkins giggle, thinking they'll sway.

The breeze whispers secrets, tickling the trees,
While the frogs croak rhymes along with the bees.
"Let's make a ruckus, with fruit on display!"
In this leafy merry-go-round, we laugh and play.

"Hello there, peach!" a loyal apple grins,
"Don't forget your roots; that's where it begins."
So the fruits unite in a dance so rare,
Creating a symphony, with nary a care.

When harvest rolls in, the fun doesn't cease,
We spin tales of laughter, and joy's released.
Amongst the roots and leaves, life's buoyant song,
In this merry embrace, we all belong.

Harvesting Whispers

The fruits they giggle in soft hues,
As squirrels plot their sneaky moves.
We climb and slip with laughter loud,
While nature watches, oh so proud.

Jars of jam or pies galore,
Each slice a secret we explore.
The juice drips down like summer rain,
A sweet, sticky mess, but who's to complain?

We dance and twirl around the plot,
Our muddy boots, a funny lot.
With every pick, a story grows,
Of sunny days and summer woes.

In the shadows, whispers blend,
Of critters plotting, making amends.
Harvest days with laughter clear,
Beneath the branches, we hold dear.

Threading Through the Thicket

Through tangled vines, we twist and shout,
As branches sway, what's that about?
An apple grin, a pear-shaped joke,
In nature's act, we're just a poke.

We wobble here, we wobble there,
Like clowns in gardens, quite the scare.
The fruit rolls free, a game of chase,
With every slip, we meet the space.

A basket full of misshapen finds,
Like thoughts unkempt, in playful minds.
Our laughter rings, a joyful song,
As bugs join in, where we belong.

Through leafy lanes, we sneak a peek,
At nature's play, so wild, so cheek.
Each giggle rumbles, crisp and clear,
In a thicket where we find cheer.

The Fruitful Silence

A quiet patch where giggles grow,
In the hush, oh how we fro.
Fruits behave like quiet jesters,
Waiting for their funny testers.

Pick one here, a woeful fall,
A sideways glance from friends in thrall.
With silly grins and silly sounds,
Our secret world beneath compounds.

A pear that rolls, a laugh divine,
Like secret notes, we twist and twine.
With every bite, a chuckle bursts,
In fruitful silence, laughter thirsts.

In the still, we hear the call,
Of nature's wit, the best of all.
The fruit, a muse, takes center stage,
In silly ways, we turn the page.

Nature's Hidden Embrace

In a corner where shadows play,
We meet the fruits in a funny way.
Like hidden gems, they slyly peek,
With each sweet taste, we laugh and speak.

Nature's hug holds tales so bright,
We stumble through with pure delight.
The branches sway, a cheeky wink,
As we balance on the brink.

The laughter echoes, sweet and loud,
With every bite, we're feeling proud.
In the orchard, where fun takes place,
All of nature joins our race.

With sticky hands and twinkling eyes,
We cherish bonds that summer ties.
In hidden ways, we find our cheer,
In nature's arms, all seem near.

Gathering the Memories

In the shade, we nibbled snacks,
Laughter echoing, what a knack!
Squirrels eyeing our feast with glee,
Plotting next to steal from me.

Bouncing balls and playful shouts,
Ticklish grass, in giggles, we spout.
A legendary pie fight ensued,
Face full of fruit—oh, how it stewed!

Old tales spat from mouths so wide,
Each story taller than the last ride.
Smudged with juice, we shared our lore,
Finding laughter on the orchard floor.

As the sun dipped, we waved goodbye,
Promising soon to return and try.
Next year the pies won't stand a chance,
For in our hearts, the fun will dance.

Camouflage of Color and Life

Underneath a leafy dome,
Colors burst, a vibrant home.
Bees make music in the air,
Even ants march without a care.

Painted fruits hang on their hooks,
Bouncing whispers from our books.
In the grass, a treasure map,
Oops! Just found a sleepy chap.

With red and green all around,
The juicy treats are newly found.
Lizard leaps in a vibrant flare,
Hiding with a cheeky glare.

Just a peek, a wiggly worm,
Nudges apples with its charm.
Who knew colors could be so bright?
In a giggle, we take flight!

Glimmers of Hope in the Orchard

Glimmers dance in daydreams bright,
Ideas bounce like rapid flight.
From branches low, we plan our rule,
A tiny kingdom made in cool.

With picnic plans on wrinkled sheets,
Imaginary creatures play with beats.
Kites fly high with colors bold,
Every story shimmering gold.

In the dusk, we share our tales,
Of cheeky kids and wobbly fails.
Each memory sprouts with silly laughs,
As the sun dips, we draft our graphs.

A wink from stars up in the sky,
Promises made—like fruit, they lie.
Hope is sweet as a pie found here,
In every moment, we spread good cheer.

Concealed Treasures of the Grove

Hidden gems in every nook,
Giggling friends and a cozy book.
Monkeys chatter from their trees,
While we find treasure in the breeze.

Apples roll like silly marbles,
Smirks emerge like playful garbles.
Case of worms playing hide-and-seek,
They creep out, oh so meek.

Laughter high as the branches sway,
Chasing critters all in play.
Footprints mark our joyful quest,
In this wonder, we're truly blessed.

Each rustle speaks of ancient lore,
In whispers soft, they urge for more.
Here, secrets hide and giggles meet,
Concealed treasures—forever sweet!

Hushed Conversations of the Wind

The wind whispers secrets, oh so sly,
As squirrels plot mischief, scampering by.
With acorns as treasure, they hide and seek,
While lazy clouds drift, cheeky and meek.

A breeze tickles branches, causing a dance,
While ants in a line take an odd little chance.
They march with a purpose, all in a row,
Who knew tiny legs could put on such a show?

Laughter is carried through rustling leaves,
As nature's comedians pull off their thieves.
A crow caws a joke, the frogs join in too,
Creating a ruckus, a humorous brew.

The wind gives a chuckle, it's time to depart,
While flowers giggle, each plays their part.
In nature's great theater, every day's grand,
With hilarity waiting just under the hand.

Boughs that Hold the Stars

Branches extend high, a stretch to the night,
A raccoon takes aim, with plans taking flight.
It aims for a star, out on a thin limb,
While others just chuckle, their laughter a hymn.

An owl's got his glasses, he reads in the tree,
A novel on nuts and a ramble with bees.
As night deepens quiet, an eerie embrace,
Frogs form a choir, all set for the chase.

Fireflies blink on, like jokes from the dark,
While hedgehogs are snorting, just adding their spark.
The leaves hold the giggles of stars shining bright,
In jokes that are shared, under soft moon's light.

When dawn draws near, and shadows retreat,
The laughter subsides, as nature knows sweet.
But hush in the branches, it waits for the day,
For comedy's cycle is never at bay.

Reverie Amongst the Leaves

In a shady spot, with the sun peeking through,
A gopher wears glasses, his thoughts about dew.
He scribbles his dreams in the soil below,
While daisies lean in, sharing tales in slow flow.

Ladybugs gossip, so brightly adorned,
As butterflies flutter with gossip reborn.
"I saw him last week!" says one in a whirl,
"Caught munching on petals, that terrible girl!"

The breeze carries chuckles, a chorus of fun,
As chipmunks race daring, in their little run.
A daydream is woven, beneath leafy suns,
With laughter encircling, in mischievous runs.

They all share a secret, as shadows grow long,
That fun is abundant, where friendship is strong.
And though day may end, here's hoping you'll find,
The laughter's not over – it's just intertwined.

Shimmering Gems of Autumn

Oh, the leaves turn to gold, what a cheerful display,
As squirrels skitter madly, collecting their hay.
With nuts tucked in pockets, they play keep away,
Wagering on who'll find the biggest bouquet.

Pumpkin pies bubbling, a sweet autumn feast,
While raccoons are sneaking, at least to say the least.
They dance around shadows, play tag with the moon,
Cackling like children, their spirit in tune.

Acorns drop softly, like applause from the sky,
While birds chirp their stories, from high up on high.
They gossip of harvests and breadcrumbs galore,
Creating a banquet that none can ignore.

When the day turns to twilight and night takes a bow,
The critters all gather, no need for a vow.
For autumn is funny; it tickles with glee,
As whispers of gems dance in laughter's decree.

Conversations with the Wind and Fruit

The wind whispers secrets, a tickle on skin,
While fruit chimes in laughter, thick as the grin.
"Did you hear that?" the apple proudly boasts,
"I'm the sweetest of all, just ask any host!"

The pear rolls its eyes, with a chuckle, it sighs,
"You're just full of seeds, I'm the one with the prize!"
The breeze tips its hat, as it swirls on a spree,
"You both look so ripe, let's just agree to be free!"

Grapes hang in clusters, swinging low with delight,
"We're the party, dear friends, let's dance through the night!"
The cherries all giggle, their laughter so sweet,
"With every good joke, we'll make life a treat!"

As laughter rolls on, they spin tales of the sun,
How laughter and joy make the sweetest of fun.
The wind takes a bow, and the fruit just can't wait,
To share all their tales at the very first date!

The Weight of Juicy Memories

Oh, the memories linger, so heavy, yet light,
Of wasps and of worms in the glow of twilight.
A splash of a peach, a tumble, a fall,
"I repeat, let's not climb, or we might lose it all!"

Lemons roll over, grumbling under their weight,
"All this zest for the past is hard to relate!"
"We've all got our stories," the oranges cry out,
"Let's toast to the times when we'd dance and just shout!"

But raspberries wink, in a cheeky parade,
"It's the weight of our laughter that never will fade!"
While blackberries murmur of secrets and grace,
"Nestle deep in the shade, it's a comfy embrace!"

As memories mingle, they plot for the next,
"Let's tell of the days when we shined at our best!"
Through giggles and grins, they lift up a cheer,
In the weight of this fruitiness, joy draws us near!

Sunlit Reveries of the Grove

The sun spills its laughter, a warm golden glow,
While shadows do jiggle, all putting on show.
"What's a fruit without sun?" a fig says with glee,
"I'm bathed in this warmth, I'm as happy as can be!"

The lemons all gossip, with zest in their tone,
"Did you hear the cute turnips have just moved in, alone?"

With peeks through the leaves, the news travels fast,
"The grove's now a stage, where the best times are cast!"

The dancing of petals, the rustle of leaves,
Yet still they complain of the mischievous thieves.
"Watch for the squirrels! They just won't take a break!"
The plums roll their eyes, plotting tricks that they make.

Amidst all the laughter, the banter, the cheer,
Each fruit shares a story, a twinkle, a tear.
In this sunlit grove, where delight never dies,
Every glance at the trees brings a fresh, fruity surprise!

Secrets of the Fruitful Shade

In the shade where the whispers bring secrets anew,
With the fruits like a chorus, resplendent in hue.
"What thoughts do you hide?" the cantaloupe hums,
"Our stories are tasty, let's see where it numbs!"

A peach pricks up ears, with a soft, juicy smile,
"I've seen things you'd gasp at, if only a while!"
The cherries all gather, so cozy and tight,
"Come spill all your secrets, we'll share them tonight!"

The shade wraps them snugly, a comfort profound,
As whispers of laughter float up from the ground.
"The pragmatics of fruit, the gossip, the style!"
"We're ripe for a riot, so let's take a while!"

So they share all their dreams, dreams big and small,
Of picnics and cakes, where there's plenty for all.
In this fruitful enclave, where giggles invade,
Secrets flourish and bloom, in the cool, leafy shade!

www.ingramcontent.com/pod-product-compliance
Lightning Source LLC
Chambersburg PA
CBHW070005300426
43661CB00141B/221